A Woman's Journal of Hopes, Dreams & Desires

NAME:

_____

DATE:

_____

S t e w a r t ,   T a b o r i   &   C h a n g

gift

Illustrations copyright © 1997 Kari Alberg
Text copyright © 1997 Jan Borene

Published in 1997 and distributed in the U.S. by
Stewart, Tabori & Chang,
a division of U.S. Media Holdings, Inc.
115 West 18th Street, New York, NY 10011

Distributed in Canada by General Publishing Co., Ltd.
30 Lesmill Road, Don Mills, Ontario, Canada M3B 2T6
Distributed in Australia by Peribo Pty Ltd.
58 Beaumont Road, Mount Kuring-gai, NSW 2080, Australia
Distributed in all other territories by Grantham Book Services, Ltd.
Isaac Newton Way, Alma Park Industrial Estate, Grantham, Lincs, NG31 9SD, England

CREATIVE DIRECTION: EEBOO CORPORATION, NYC • DESIGNER: BRENDA BROWN FORTUNATO

ISBN: 1-55670-725-8

PRINTED IN CHINA

2 4 6 8 9 7 5 3

Hope sleeps in our bones like a bear
waiting for spring to rise and walk.

MARGE PIERCY,
Stone, Paper, Knife

And learning that what we must do with our "love forever; hate never" dreams is — let them go.

JUDITH VIORST,
Necessary Losses

Name a precious dream that you had to let go. What are some ways you have dealt with the loss and grief around this dream?

To break the moulds, to be heedless of the seductions of security is an impossible struggle, but one of the few that count.

ROBYN DAVIDSON,
Tracks

Which types of security are pulls for you? Money? Relationships? Geography? Family? Friends? Career? After listing them, rate their pull on a 1-10 scale, with 10 being the strongest.

. . . the fierce independence that was suddenly mine,

to remain inside me no matter how

it scared me when I tumbled, was an inheritance.

EUDORA WELTY,
One Writer's Beginnings

Which relatives or other important people from your past displayed "fierce independence"? In what ways has that influenced you?

Not the destination, but the willingness to wander in pursuit characterizes pilgrimage.

PATRICIA HAMPL,
Spillville

Describe a time when you were unsure where you were headed, though in retrospect you realize that you gained something valuable from the journey.

I can't do it, you say it's killing me,
but you thrive, you glow
on the street like a neon raspberry.

MARGE PIERCY,
The Moon Is Always Female

Remember a time when you were ready to give up but went ahead anyway
and felt energized when you finished. Describe in detail the feelings you
had at your lowest point before the breakthrough, and your feelings after.

We must come to live within the shifting ambiguities of being both good and bad, wise and foolish, fortunate and unfortunate.

SHELDON KOPP,
An End to Innocence

What personality trait do you have that can be considered both an asset and a liability? Describe a situation in which this trait has been positive and one in which it has been negative.

The struggle for one's self is not easy and demands the development of inner strength and self-conviction. It comes with love.

KAYLAN PICKFORD,
Always a Woman

Finish this thought with as many endings as you can:
I wish I had the courage to . . .

*Fear becomes an ally which whispers that we
are coming to our edge, to unplumbed depths,
to the space in which all growth occurs.*

STEPHEN LEVINE,
Healing into Life and Death

Recall a time in your life when you were fearful of an outcome. What
were you afraid would happen? How did things actually turn out?

*Now I am in a blind alley with all doors closed to hope,
and I don't know how to handle so much fear.*

ISABEL ALLENDE,
Paula

When you are deeply afraid, what are some of the ways
you take care of yourself to move through the fear?

We like knowing what is to happen
with small surprises. But sometimes
we must endure or create gross shocks
that stretch us till we grow or break.

MARGE PIERCY,
Stone, Paper, Knife

Remember a time when something suddenly and dramatically changed in your life. What are some positive outcomes from that change? What are some negatives?

I reached beyond what I thought were my limits to become part of my life on my own merits, by my own strength, and in my own time.

KAYLAN PICKFORD,
Always a Woman

When have you exceeded your limits to get through something or achieve something? What kinds of inner and outer support helped you at this time?

The child and girl I was, the woman I am,
the old woman I shall be,
are all water in the same rushing torrent.

ISABEL ALLENDE,
Paula

What are some of the positive words you would use
to describe yourself as a child? How have these
qualities continued to be a part of your adult life?

We may be a long time learning that life is, at best, "a dream controlled" — that reality is built of imperfect connections.

JUDITH VIORST,
Necessary Losses

Finish the following sentence with as many endings as you can rapidly write:
My life would be different if . . .

The question to ask is not whether
you are a success or a failure, but whether
you are a learner or a nonlearner.

CAROLE HYATT AND LINDA GOTTLIEB,
When Smart People Fail

Think of a time when you have labeled yourself as a success or
a failure. Now write what you learned from either experience.

I have found that it is the willingness to say what I feel and want that makes me feel whole.

SHAKTI GAWAIN,
Living in the Light

Do this exercise quickly. Finish these sentences:

      I wish I were more... ·

      I would love to...

      I am afraid of...

      I feel most content when...

      If I had another chance, I would...

Passionate investment leaves us vulnerable to loss. And sometimes, no matter how clever we are, we must lose.

JUDITH VIORST,
Necessary Losses

Have you attempted something that did not turn out as you hoped, despite your best efforts? Write a letter to yourself praising all that you tried, and reassure yourself that some outcomes are out of your control.

Our strength is in our dreams, and those who do not dare to dream damn themselves.

MERLE SHAIN,
Hearts That We Broke Long Ago

What is the most unrealistic, unattainable fantasy or daydream you have? Include details of where and how you would live, what you would look like, what you would have achieved, etc. Be outrageous.

It is an act of courage to acknowledge our own uncertainty and sit with it for a while.

HARRIET GOLDHOR LERNER,
The Dance of Anger

Identify an issue about which you feel ambivalence. Explore how it would feel to allow yourself simply to experience the uncertainty and confusion for one week, without trying to come to a decision. Would this be difficult?

The Chinese word for "crisis" is the same as the word for "opportunity" — a rather brilliant linguistic marriage.

CAROLE HYATT AND LINDA GOTTLIEB,
When Smart People Fail

Draw a line down the center of the page. Write "Crisis" at the top of one side and "Opportunity" at the top of the other. Make a list of crises, past or present, and another list of opportunities they created or may create.

Notice what happens when you follow your intuitive feelings. The result is usually increased energy and power, and a sense of things flowing.

SHAKTI GAWAIN,
Living in the Light

Remember a time when you trusted your intuition. Did you feel a surge of energy? Was this a pleasant, exhilarating feeling?

... happiness not only needs no justification,
but ... it is also the only final test of whether
what I am doing is right for me.

JOANNA FIELD,
A Life of One's Own

Make a quick "not-thinking" list of activities that bring you joy. After
you have finished the list, write next to each item when you last did it.

Courage is not the absence of fear;

it is the making of action in spite of fear.

M. SCOTT PECK,
The Road Less Traveled

Write down one of your worst fears. Take a few minutes, then write
some possible scenarios that might occur after your worst fear came
true. Include both positive and negative outcomes.

Grief is the rope burns left behind when what
we have held to most dearly is
pulled out of reach, beyond our grasp.

STEPHEN LEVINE,
Healing into Life and Death

Have you had a precious hope or dream dashed? What was it?
What has helped you handle the grief of losing this dream? What
parts still feel tender around this loss?

If we have not achieved our early dreams,

we must either find new ones

or see what we can salvage from the old.

ROSALYNN CARTER,
Something to Gain

Have you let go of a dream that was important to you? What are some elements of that early dream that could be rewoven into a new dream?

The glory of a dream is this — that it despises facts, and makes its own. Our dream saves us from going mad; that is enough.

OLIVE SCHREINER,
The Story of an African Farm, Part II

Recall a time when, in spite of discouragement from others, you followed a dream, even if it did not succeed. What types of negative things did others say? How do you feel about pursuing that dream now?

I believe in some blending of hope and sunshine sweetening the worst lots.

CHARLOTTE BRONTË,
Villette

Whom can you turn to when times are difficult? Do these people lighten your load? Who turns to you when they need someone to soften a hard time?

It's exhilarating to be alive in a time of awakening consciousness; it can also be confusing, disorienting, and painful.

ADRIENNE RICH,
"When We Dead Awaken;
Writing as Re-Vision"

What are some of the feelings you enjoy during a decision-making process? What are some of the feelings you find uncomfortable?

But the biggest problem of map-making is not that we have to start from scratch, but that if our maps are to be accurate we have to continually revise them.

M. SCOTT PECK,
The Road Less Traveled

When you were younger where did you think your life would be at this age? What are some of the revisions you have made so far on your map? Which revisions are you happy with, and which do you question today?

Hopes are what your waking mind can imagine. Like prayers. Like bridges you can cross to a better place.

MARSHA NORMAN,
The Fortune Teller

Write down some of your current, deepest hopes that seem to have no resolution as yet. Just name them. Now take a walk or a nap, cook something, listen to music. Let your hopes be for now.

Dreams pass into the reality of action.

From the action stems the dream again; and this interdependence produces the highest form of living.

ANAÏS NIN,
The Diary of Anaïs Nin

Follow the thread of some dream that you have put into action that led to another dream and more action, and so on. Are you currently in a dream part or an action part of this trail? Are you in both?

*We always attract into our lives whatever we
think about most, believe in most strongly, expect on
the deepest level, and imagine most vividly.*

SHAKTI GAWAIN,
Reflections in the Light

Describe in detail something you deeply want. How will it look? Imagine
you have already attained it. Write about how your dream became real as
though you were writing to a friend you have not talked to in years.

The very least you can do in your life is
      to figure out what you hope for. And the most
you can do is live inside that hope.

BARBARA KINGSOLVER,
Animal Dreams

Ignoring what other people may think unrealistic, what are
some things you hope for in your life? If that sounds too big
to handle, what is one thing you hope will happen today?

*The need for change bulldozed a road
down the center of my mind.*

MAYA ANGELOU,
I Know Why the Caged Bird Sings

Remember a time in your life when you felt strongly and clearly that the moment had come for a big change. Describe the physical and emotional feelings you experienced.

Some women wait for something

to change and nothing

does change

so they change

themselves.

AUDRE LORD,
"Stations"

What are some words other people have used to describe you? Which words or traits do you like? Which ones make you uncomfortable?

Courage can't see around corners,
but goes around them anyway.

MIGNON MCLAUGHLIN,
The Neurotic's Notebook

Choose an aspect of your life that you would most like to change.
After writing it down, quickly write a list of single words that come
to mind when you think of actually making this change.

Many of us are frightened by the unknown.
Yet deep within us all are reserves of strength
and courage that can lead us on.

CLAUDIA PANUTHOS AND CATHERINE ROMEO,
Ended Beginnings

What are some feelings or consequences you are hoping to
avoid by not making a change that you know in your heart
must be made? Write yourself a note of support.

It took me a long time to learn that doing what nourished my spirit was not selfish, but essential.

KAYLAN PICKFORD,
Always a Woman

What is a cherished activity you do for yourself? Are there times you feel guilty for taking the time for this activity? What would you like to do that you have not done because of fears of being labeled selfish?

I suppose you can't have everything, though my instinctive response to this sentiment is always, "Why not?"

MARGARET HALSEY,
Some of My Best Friends are Soldiers

Imagine you have just called you best friend for help on deciding whether or not to make a scary change in your life. Now write yourself a letter of encouragement as though it were being written to you by your friend.

Dreams are the only

afterlife we know;

the place where the children

we were

rock in the arms of the children

we have become

LINDA PASTAN,
"Dreams"

Write a description of yourself when you were twelve or thirteen—what you looked like, who your friends were, what you liked to do. What are some things you love to do now that are as much fun as the things you did at that age?

There is no such thing as expecting too much.

SUSAN CHEEVER,
Looking for Work

Describe an ideal room of your own. Furniture? Colors?
Objects? Sounds? Views? Size? Lighting? Windows?
What do you enjoy doing in this room?

Our wishes never seem so little desirable as when on the verge of accomplishment; we draw back instinctively, they look so different from what we expected.

GERALDINE JEWSBURY,
Zoë

Can you recall something you wanted desperately, only to find the experience unsatisfying when you attained it? Write what your expectations were and how you actually felt upon reaching your goal.

My expectations — which I extended whenever
I came close to accomplishing my goals — made it
impossible ever to feel satisfied with my success.

ELLEN SUE STERN,
The Indispensable Woman

Do you allow yourself space for enjoying your
successes? Take time now to make a list of things
you have accomplished and feel proud of achieving.

It is sometimes hard to recognize life's offerings.

They can come in strange disguises.

KAYLAN PICKFORD,
Always a Woman

Can you remember a time when you had a "blessing in disguise"? How quickly did you recognize it as a blessing? Is there a difficult part of your life now that has the potential to be perceived as a blessing later?

How extraordinary people are, that they get themselves into such situations where they go on doing what they dislike doing, and have no need or obligation to do, simply because it seems to be expected.

MARGARET DRABBLE,
The Middle Ground

Which tasks are you looking forward to doing today or tomorrow?
Which ones are you dreading? Choose one task you dislike that is
not truly essential and do not do it for one day.

Expect nothing. Live frugally

On surprise

ALICE WALKER,
"Expect Nothing"

Do you consider yourself more rational or intuitive when making major decisions? If you are both, describe the situations that bring out each side.

Faith is not being sure. It is not being sure,
but betting with your last cent.

MARY JEAN IRION,
Yes, World

Imagine a conversation with someone you admire deeply, living or
not, fictional or real. Ask this person for his or her advice on an issue
with which you are struggling. Write down this advice to you.

Faith is what makes life bearable, with all its tragedies and ambiguities and sudden, startling joys.

MADELEINE L'ENGLE,
Walking on Water

What are some sources of faith for you? Where do you go or what do you do when you experience a tragic loss or are deeply afraid? How and where do you express gratitude when life is kind to you?

Suddenly many movements are going on within me,
many things are happening, there is
an almost unbearable sense of sprouting, of bursting
encasements, of moving kernels, expanding flesh.

MERIDEL LE SUEUR,
"Annunciation"

What is your favorite season of the year? What are the feelings and activities you like about that time? At what time of day do you feel the most energy? What would you like to do at that time if you could do anything?

I used to think there would be a blinding flash of light someday, and then I would be wise and calm and would know how to cope with everything...

MARGARET LAURENCE,
The Fire-Dwellers

Is there an aspect of your life in which you still cling to the belief that there is one right answer, one you just have not yet found? Write about how hard it is to be an adult some days, when you realize that no one really has all the answers.

I could never tell where inspiration begins and impulse leaves off. . . . If your hunch proves a good one, you were inspired; if it proves bad, you are guilty of yielding to thoughtless impulse.

BERYL MARKHAM,
West with the Night

Name an important life decision in your past. Write about the time before you made the decision. Was it impulsive or long and agonizing? Did your friends support you? Do you beat yourself up if your choice turns out badly?

It is only by following your deepest instinct that you can lead a rich life and if you let your fear of consequence prevent you from following your deepest instinct, then your life will be safe, expedient and thin.

KATHERINE BUTLER HATHAWAY,
The Journals and Letters of the Little Locksmith

Name someone who has been supportive of your daring side. How does she or he show their support? Write a thank you note to him or her, even if you do not or cannot send it.

I believe that we are always attracted to
what we need most, an instinct leading us towards
the persons who are to open new vistas in
our lives and fill them with new knowledge.

HELENE ISWOLSKY,
Light Before Dusk

Do you have a supportive network of friends or family? Make a list of some of your favorite people, past and present, who have been there for you in the rough times. Can you also remember a time that someone seemed to appear at just the right time with just the right connection for you, either personally or professionally?

I'm the breathless woman

I'm the hurried woman

I'm the girl with the unquenchable thirst

ANNE WALDMAN,
"Fast Speaking Woman"

When was a time you felt an almost unstoppable passion
for something? Was this a positive or frightening feeling?
Were you able to follow that passion?

Nothing is ever quite as bad as it could be.

AMY HEMPEL,
At the Gates of the Animal Kingdom

Let yourself go on this one. Conjure up the worst possible scenario you can imagine involving something that is worrying you. Take a deep breath. Now make it even worse. Keep going until you run out of paper.

Some folks are natural born kickers.

They can always find a way to turn disaster into butter.

KATHERINE PATTERSON,
Lyddie

Describe someone you admire, real or fictional, who often seems to turn disaster in his or her life into something positive. What specific traits does he or she have that you also have or would like to have?

Leaps over walls—especially when taken late in life— can be extremely perilous. To leap successfully, you need a sense of humor, the spirit of adventure and an unshakable conviction that what you are leaping over is an obstacle upon which you would otherwise fall down.

MONICA BALDWIN,
I Leap over the Wall

Think of someone in your past who was discouraging whenever you wanted to try something new. Is this voice still dancing around in your head when you are considering a new venture? Write down what she or he would say to you about something you want to try now. Write a response to her or him, imagining that you are completely clear and confident about your actions.

A new beatitude I write for thee,

"Blessed are they who are not sure of things."

JULIA C. R. DORR,
"A New Beatitude"

Quickly write down several things in your life about which you are unsure. Take a few moments. Then write out the phrase "Blessed are they who are not sure of things" three times.

The only thing that makes life possible is permanent, intolerable uncertainty: not knowing what comes next.

URSULA K. LEGUIN,
The Left Hand of Darkness

Finish this sentence: What I like about not knowing the future is...

If you do nothing unexpected, nothing unexpected happens.

FAY WELDON,
Moon over Minneapolis

What are some activities that you would like to do, that would startle people who know you? Imagine you have done one of these things. What have you done, and how are your friends reacting? What are some of the things they might say?

The cream of enjoyment in this life is always impromptu. The chance walk; the unexpected visit; the unpremeditated journey; the unsought conversation or acquaintance.

FANNY FERN,
Caper Sauce

Does being playful and spontaneous come easily to you? If so, what are some of your favorite impulsive adventures? If not, is this something you would like to change, or are you comfortable as you are?

Every trip had held an element of disaster,
every new adventure had had a point where it
looked meaningless, and every person I met seemed a
little strange. But it had all added up to something...

DEBBY BULL,
Blue Jelly

Write about a time that you literally or figuratively took
a wrong turn, or your plans went awry, and the twists
and turns resulted in something wonderful happening.

But I feel too spread out now, like I've been

rolled out with a rolling pin and

I can't gather myself in to focus on anything.

JANE SMILEY,
Ordinary Love & Good Will

Pretend you have a whole day to pamper yourself.
Money is no object and you can be anywhere in the
world. Where would you go? What would you do?

My first thoughts were of the peculiar inner contentment.
. . . This feeling had a quality of goodness about it,
like the "goodness" of a cat lying in the sun.

JOANNA FIELD,
An Experiment in Leisure

When was the last time you felt serene and centered?
What were your surroundings? Were you alone or
with people? How long ago was this time?

personal reflections

personal reflections

personal reflections

personal reflections

personal reflections

personal reflections

personal reflections

personal reflections

personal reflections